Praise for
The Sex Lives of College Students

In *The Sex Lives of College Students,* Dr. Sandy Caron provides an important glimpse into the sexual lives and attitudes of college students, both today and as compared with 25 years ago. Her analysis is spot on, as she reflects on findings in light of children and youth being raised in a society that is both sex saturated and sex silent.

We "don't talk about it" at home, school, house of worship, or in the doctor's office. So young people are guided by sexually explicit media, i.e. pornography, as the education about what sex looks like. More students are faking orgasms, nearly all, like the porn stars, shave all their pubic hair, and the double standard still lives on. At the same time, today's students are more tolerant, e.g. of LGBT friends, and females can have "friends with benefits," thus having casual sex in ways males have historically done.

Of particular note for this sexual scholar trained by the late Dr. Sol Gordon, who championed parents as the first and in many ways more important sex educators of their children, 54% had asked their mother a question or two, while 75% had never asked their father any questions about sex.

We can do better to prepare young people for their adult lives as sexual beings. Dr. Caron's highly accessible "viewbook" tells us what is, which may well help with needed education about sexual health, relationships, and pleasure.

— Betsy Crane, Ph.D.
Professor, Center for Human Sexuality Studies, Widener University

• •

How do college students experience and express their sexualities? Has this changed over time? Here we find painless statistics, no boring numbers! New generations of college students, seeking to personally solve the mysteries of sex and sexuality, will find their answers here in a colorful, compelling, easy-to-comprehend format. Their parents will be interested, too. As a sexuality researcher myself, I have great appreciation for the information Dr. Sandy Caron has compiled and how she has presented it.

— Carol Rinkleib Ellison, Ph.D.
AASECT certified sexuality educator and therapist,
and author of *Women's Sexualities. Generations of Women Share Intimate Secrets of Sexual Self Acceptance*

Praise for *The Sex Lives of College Students*

In an age when rampant misinformation about sex permeates the airwaves, television screens, and movie houses of America, Sandy Caron pulls us back into reality-- one filled not with pompous sexual 'achievement,' but with sexual insecurities, gender inequities, contradiction, paradox, and clear places to celebrate and to worry, especially for supposed advances in women's sexual liberation. An enjoyable, accessible read that will delight anyone wanting a clear look at undergraduate sexuality across time."

— Breanne Fahs, Ph.D.
Associate Professor of Women and Gender Studies
at Arizona State University
Author of *Performing Sex and The Moral Panics of Sexuality*

• •

The Sex Lives of College Students provides a snapshot of young adult sexual behavior over the past 25 years as well as an analysis of trends over that same time period. The outstanding graphic design of the book makes for very easy information processing. It is a quick read, yet provides a great deal of useful, scientifically-based information in a more comprehensive way than many longer and more detailed resources on sexual behavior and attitudes.

— Terri D. Fisher, Ph.D.
Professor of Psychology and Assistant Dean
The Ohio State University at Mansfield

• •

Sandra Caron's excellent new book, *The Sex Lives of College Students*, is a significant and essential addition to our understanding of human sexuality. This is solid, scientific research presented in a compelling and enjoyable format. *The Sex Lives of College Students* entertains while expanding our insights into young adults' sexual behaviors, thoughts, and feelings, today and over the past 25 years. Dr. Caron's contribution to the field is sure to have a lasting influence for decades to come. This book is a must-read for educators; researchers; current and prospective college students; and parents.

— Roger R. Hock, Ph.D.
Professor of Psychology at Mendocino College
Author of the college textbook, *Human Sexuality, 4th Edition*,
Forty Studies that Changed Psychology, 7th Edition, and
*It's My Life Now: Starting Over After an Abusive Relationship or Domestic Violence,
2nd Edition* (with Meg Kennedy Dugan)

Praise for *The Sex Lives of College Students*

For decades, we've been stuck with fact-free magazine polls, misguided myths, non-representative psychology studies, and just plain wild guesses about what college students actually do sexually. Now we finally know, thanks to years of hard work by Dr. Sandra Caron. Based on reliable data from thousands of students, her new book *The Sex Lives of College Students* tells us what they do, what they think they do, why they think they do it, and how they like it. This is a funny, serious, insightful, surprising, and ultimately reassuring book. It's easy to read, hard to put down, and a wonderful conversation-starter between mates, parents and adolescents, or people just starting a relationship. I've admired Sandy's teaching for years. Now I admire her writing as well.

— Marty Klein, Ph.D.
Sex therapist and author of
Sexual Intelligence: What We Really Want From Sex, and How to Get It
(HarperCollins)

• •

Has anything related to sex behavior changed in the past twenty-five years? The quick answer most would give is "of course"! How do we know? And has it changed in a sexually healthy way? *The Sex Lives of College Students* provides a unique look over time of what many of us wonder, given the media presentation of values and images. 'Sex Lives' is a HUGE "gold mine" in a very small package. Wonderful visuals, and presentation of data. Yes... "data" that is fun to read and can be used with adults and youth alike to stimulate important conversations.

— Konstance McCaffree, Ph.D., CSE, CFLE
President AASECT (American Association of Sexuality Educators, Counselors & Therapists) AASECT Certified Sexuality Educator
Sexuality Consultant, Adjunct Professor Widener University

• •

Facts about sex can launch life-changing discussions. *The Sex Lives of College Students* highlights hundreds of issues we're all curious about—from safe sex, oral sex, and sexual self-esteem, to orgasms, faking orgasms, and much more. The lively Q-A format offers upbeat, updated information to help students debunk myths and half-truths, and pave their way to becoming savvy, confident lovers and partners.

— Gina Ogden, Ph.D., LMFT
Author: *Expanding the Practice of Sex Therapy and The Return of Desire*

Praise for *The Sex Lives of College Students*

The Sex Lives of College Students is a sexual health bible. Imagine having a window with a view of the sexual attitudes and behavior of 5,606 students. Some of the most unspoken sexual health issues are presented clearly for all to see and process. If our goal is to have young people understand their own sexuality and make healthy sexual decisions this is a must read for high school and college students and their parents.

— Mark Schoen, Ph.D.
Founder, SexSmartFilms.com
Producer, Transthemovie.com

• •

The Sex Lives of College Students is a uniquely impressive and intriguing bird's eye view into the world of young people. Dr. Caron's findings – gathered from more than 25 years of research – will not only inform the work of college professors teaching human sexuality, but also serves as a blueprint for secondary education teachers and public health policy makers as they prepare their teaching and intervention priorities, as well as parents, as they prepare the conversations that are necessary and relevant.

Bill Taverner, MA, CSE
Executive Director, The Center for Sex Education
Editor-in-Chief, *American Journal of Sexuality Education*

• •

Dr. Caron's book will allow conversations about who is doing what with whom - and telling whom -- and thinking what -- to be based on Maine college student data instead of pundits' imaginations. Hallelujah. Facts are a rare breath of fresh air when it comes to sex. Now let's have a few people in the South and West and big cities replicate this heroic effort -- if only!

— Leonore Tiefer, Ph.D.
Clinical Associate Professor of Psychiatry, NYU School of Medicine
Founder, New View Campaign

Second
Edition

THE SEX LIVES OF COLLEGE STUDENTS:

A quarter century of attitudes and behaviors

Sandra Caron, Ph.D.

Foreword by Dr. Clive Davis

Illustrated by Val Ireland

Acknowledgement

Some of my best teachers have been my students. I want to thank all the college students who took the time to respond to the human sexuality survey in order to provide us with greater insight and understanding.

Designed by Val Ireland

Printed in the United States of America

ISBN-13: 978-0-9912601-3-3
Maine College Press, Inc
P.O. Box 351
Orono, ME 04473

SexLivesofCollegeStudents.com

Contents

Twenty-Five Year Data Set

Sexual Behaviors

Newer Data Set

Foreword

by Clive M. Davis, Ph.D.

Emeritus Associate Professor of Psychology, Syracuse University
Past President of the Society for the Scientific Study of Sexuality
Past President of the Foundation for the Scientific Study of Sexuality
Former Editor of *The Journal of Sex Research*

I met Dr. Sandra (Sandy) Caron more than 30 years ago when she came to my office at Syracuse University to introduce herself. She told me about her work as an undergraduate at the University of Maine and her plans to pursue a doctoral program at Syracuse University. Over the course of our conversation, we discovered that we shared a scientific interest in understanding the sexual attitudes and behaviors of our countrymen and women, and in sharing that knowledge with our students through formal coursework and peer educational programs. We also learned that we were both "Mainers," having grown up in towns only a few miles from one another (although our "growing up" was a generation or so apart). Thus, we found we "spoke the same language" in more ways than one. And we Mainers can be different! Since that first meeting, I have learned much more about Sandy, and we have shared much together, ultimately becoming colleagues and friends. I am honored and pleased to be able to say a word to two about Sandy and this book, *The Sex Lives of College Students*.

No one has collected comparable data over such a long time span. As you will see, these "snapshots" are often fascinating, especially if we look at them in relation to other trends in our culture over this same period of time.

First, the book. The contents derive from more than 25 years of data obtained from an annual survey of college students enrolled in Sandy's basic human sexuality course at the University of Maine. The study is unique. Nearly 6,000 students have answered the survey questions. Thus, the results offer considerable insight into the attitudes and behaviors of a diverse group of young adults, at specific points in time — and over time. Although the data are not longitudinal in the statistical sense (i.e., comparing the same people over time), the similarities and the differences between and among the groups over the years are instructive, suggesting changes that may have occurred over time.

No one has collected comparable data over such a long time span. As you will see, these "snapshots" are often fascinating, especially if we look at them in relation to other trends in our culture over this same period of time. Are the results representative of our society at large? Again, we cannot be sure, but they are certainly suggestive, given the consistencies in the data. The results are also valuable in another way: For the students who provided the answers to questions about their beliefs, attitudes and behavior, the results offered them a perspective, helping them understand their own sexualities in the context of their generation. In addition, they — and we who are the readers of this book — can gain insight into the sexualities of those students, as well as our own.

Sandy Caron is also unique. All of us are, of course, but some of us are more unique than others. The mere fact that Sandy had the foresight to collect — systematically — this large body of data over this lengthy period of time is remarkable. Many of us who have taught large human sexuality courses have used surveys of our students' beliefs, attitudes and behaviors, but few of us have had the foresight, the determination and the persistence to do so systematically over 25 years. Furthermore, almost no one has compiled and analyzed his or her data in such a way that the findings contribute to our knowledge about similarities and differences between groups of people (e.g., men compared to women) — and over time. Perhaps the most important characteristic of Sandy's personality is her enthusiasm. She is a great teacher because she is involved and committed, and convinces students that they, too, can be invested in learning about themselves and others. She makes learning fun. Enjoy her, as I have, through her work.

— Clive M. Davis, Ph.D.

Introduction

**What do nearly 6,000 college
students have to say about sex?**

What do they do?

What do they think?

How do they feel about it?

**How has the media and Internet
influenced their actions?**

**Compared to 25 years ago,
is sex really different today?**

n this second edition of *The Sex Lives of College Students*
results are presented of a human sexuality survey
administered over the past quarter century (from
1990–2015) to thousands of college students ages 18–80.
Responses by 5,606 college students between the ages of
18–22 are compiled here. Many of the questions originated
from a survey administered in the 1970s and 1980s by the
world-renowned sexuality educator, Dr. Sol Gordon at
Syracuse University. As my mentor and advisor for my
doctoral degree in human sexuality, Dr. Gordon encouraged
me to continue to distribute the survey in my own human
sexuality classes when I became a faculty member at the
University of Maine.

The more than 100-question survey has been administered during the first week of every human sexuality class at the University of Maine since 1990. The undergraduate class has a capacity enrollment of 350 students and regular waiting lists. In 2010, several new questions were added and refined to address the latest issues and trends, including the use of social media to facilitate relationships and use of morning-after pills.

Above all, the findings raise awareness about students' understanding of sex matters

The goal is to survey college students' attitudes and behaviors at the start of the course. And while many of the students enrolled in the human sexuality course are majoring in the social sciences, the students represent every college and major at the university.

Many take the popular class as an elective to "unlearn what they've learned." For all, the academically rigorous class is also a personal journey, helping them learn how to be comfortable talking about sex and their sexuality.

The survey results are shared with the class to demonstrate the value of sex research and to serve as a springboard for discussions. The students are able to compare themselves to other studies of college sexual attitudes and behaviors, as well as to results from previous students completing the survey. Above all, the findings raise awareness about students' understanding of sex matters (e.g., despite an image of college life involving sex every weekend, nearly half the respondents say they have gone a few months without sex) and difficult issues (nearly a third of the students surveyed responded that they have had an involuntary sexual experience, and more than half the students know someone who had been raped).

In many cases, the survey data help students let go of "bedtime fables" — such misconceptions as "bigger is better" and the misconception that everyone knows the secrets to sex. The latter is particularly detrimental when men and women find themselves disappointed in their relationships when their sexual partners fail to satisfy them.

Among the most telling disparities between perceptions and reality: the question about faking orgasms. Despite the 1960s Sexual Revolution and what appears to be more openness than ever before concerning relationships, the data found that a quarter of men and two-thirds of women say they have faked orgasms and that number has gone up — not down — over the 25 years. Those numbers tell us that we've lost touch with what sexual relationships are supposed to be about — enjoying ourselves rather than faking pleasure and satisfaction.

Similarly, the lower number of women who said they masturbate (only two-thirds of women compared to nearly 100 percent of men) speaks to the failure to know ourselves and what turns us on. And without that self-knowledge, how can we tell a partner what feels good/what we prefer?

Those survey responses tell us we still have a long way to go before people own their sexuality. The survey reinforces the fact that young adults are generally comfortable pursuing sexual relationships, but often fail to openly discuss sexual issues. What's needed is the confidence of sexual partners to engage in honest conversations about what pleasures them most. Some of the results suggest that the double standard is alive and well when we see that college men are more likely to inflate the number of sex partners they have had, while more women underreport; and college women are much more likely to say love is important in sex, while many men say love is not important at all.

The survey also shows progress in a number of areas, including greater acceptance of sexual diversity and awareness of the importance of safer sex and sexual responsibility, which has resulted in lower numbers of STIs and abortions.

The Sex Lives of College Students raises awareness, addresses the issues and provides perspective on the trends through the past quarter century in the sex lives of college students.

In this, the age of the Internet, young adults contend they are informed and free of the guilt and hang ups of their parents' generations, yet most college students have many questions regarding sex. While some know how to proactively get accurate answers to their questions, or had good sex education classes in high school or parents who had open, honest communication about sex, many more college students seem to have a junior high mentality when it comes to sexuality — they may not know much more than what they learned in a middle school class on puberty. With today's technology, there's a sea of accessible half-truths and misinformation about sex. The trick is to find accurate information that heightens awareness, informs decision-making, and promotes healthy lifestyles and well-being.

The survey data serve as a reality check on the sex lives of college students. Despite the perception that all college students are regularly hooking up, their survey responses indicate that, overall, they are neither feeling overly liberated sexually nor jumping into bed with multiple partners. Instead, the survey shows a range of opinions and experience in sexual relationships.

College students have lots of questions around sex and, depending on the quality — and sources — of the sex education they received as teens, some may even have some "unlearning" to do. College is such a critical time for young people making decisions about relationships. It is a time of new beginnings, changes and discoveries. It is an opportunity to be informed and be more comfortable with their bodies.

As our future leaders, it's important for them — and those who care about them — to understand and help them "own" their sexuality as part of a healthy lifestyle.

Without information, including the correct information, too many young adults end up having inflated expectations and engaging in sexual acts with little meaning. They wind up thinking that good sex is about how one looks and performs. As reflected in the media, young people live in a sex saturated but sex silent society in which there is not enough informed dialogue.

The hope is that The Sex Lives of College Students can jumpstart the dialogue.

However, this book is not the be-all and end-all survey on the sex lives of college students. It is not representative of a cross-section of all college students across the country, but it does give us a glimpse of a student sample from a mid-size public research university. Indeed, it is a unique perspective informed by a 25-year data set (spanning from 1990–2015), analyzed with the help of statistician Dr. Brian Doore of the University of Maine Office of Assessment. The data facilitate the tracking of trends and comparison of changes in attitudes and behaviors.

Because of its longevity, the survey includes not only the views of today's college students, but also those of their parents, including some who may have sat in the same lecture hall taking the course in human sexuality.

I invite you to visit The Sex Lives of College Students website (**sexlivesofcollegestudents.com**) to view the survey, and to post questions and comments to inform the next edition of the book. In addition, you can follow us on Facebook (The Sex Lives of College Students) and Twitter (#sexlivescollege).

The Demographics
The sample: 5,606 undergraduates attending the University of Maine

Age:	18–22 years
Sex:	Two-thirds women; one-third men
Year in College:	From first-year students to seniors
Race:	Most White/Non-Hispanic
Religion:	More than half Christian
Relationships:	Half in a serious relationship
Orientation:	Most self-identified as heterosexual

Sexual Behavior:

1990–2015 Data

1. Ever done it?
2. When was your first time?
3. Do you use protection?
4. Birth control of choice?
5. How many people have you been with?
6. How do you feel about the number of people you've been with?
7. Ever lied about how many people you've been with?
8. Ever faked it?
9. Ever masturbated?
10. How old were you when you started masturbating?
11. How often do you masturbate?
12. Ever had sexual experiences with someone of the same sex?

Ever done it?

College men and women were asked, "Have you ever had sexual intercourse?" Of the 5,569 who answered this question, the overwhelming majority

87% report that they have had sexual intercourse.

This is not to say there are no college virgins, but certainly there are few.

There has also been a leveling of the playing field between men and women. Despite the notion that men are more interested and more sexually active than women, there is little difference between college men and women who report having had sex (88% of men and 87% of women).

Free of parental supervision and living in co-ed residence halls with hundreds of students their same age, it is no surprise that the proportion of college students who say they have had sexual intercourse increases by class standing. In other words, the longer they are in college, the more likely they are to experience sexual intercourse. By the time they are seniors 9 out of 10 college men and women have had sex.

Results over 25 years:

In the past quarter century, **not much has changed in terms of the percentage of college students reporting that they have had sexual intercourse.** Despite more than $1.5 billion have been spent to promote abstinence-only-until-marriage "education" since the 1990s, there has been little to no change in college student behavior.

1990s to today

NO CHANGE

in % of college students having intercourse

Across all respondents, 87% (n=4,856) indicated they have had sexual intercourse.

The percentage of those who have had intercourse increased across years in college.

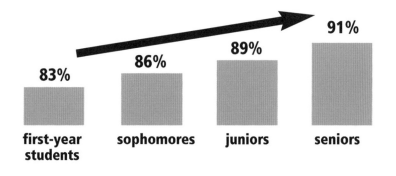

91%

89%

86%

83%

first-year students   sophomores   juniors   seniors

When was your first time?

College students were asked, "At what age did you first have sexual intercourse?"

Most college students report that their first experience with sexual intercourse occurred in high school. Of the 4,888 college students who say they have had sex, most (88%) had their first experience by age 18

typically when they were

16 – 17 years old

More women say they lost their virginity closer to age 16, while men say their first time was closer to 17.

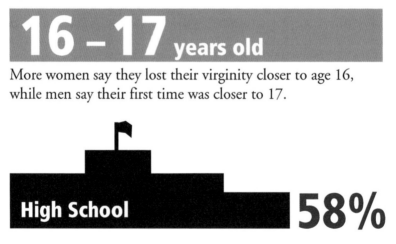

High School 58%

Results over 25 years:

Despite the perception that teens are having sex at earlier and earlier ages, the age of first intercourse has remained relatively unchanged in the past 25 years, with most experiencing first intercourse at age 16 or 17.

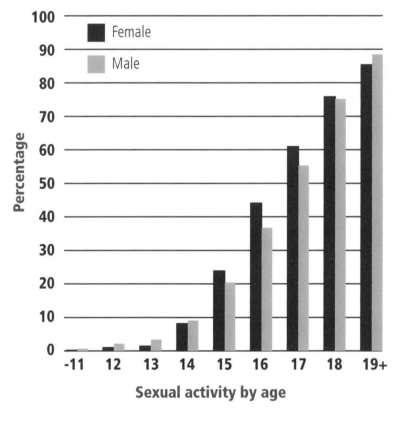

Looking at the percent who say they lost their virginity in their teen years reveals the dramatic increase in sexual activity

Do you use protection?

College men and women who have had sexual intercourse were asked, "If you had sexual intercourse during the past three months, did you or your partner use birth control every time?"

The good news is the majority of the 4,199 students who say they had sex in the last three months

82% affirm that they used birth control every time.

On the down side, this means nearly

1:5 did not

YesYes YesYes No Yes YesYes Yes No

Results over 25 years:

The other piece of good news is that over the past 25 years, **there has been an increase in the number of college students who say they use birth control every time.** Reports of birth control use have increased from approximately 75% in the early 1990s to nearly 85% of today's students saying they use it every time.

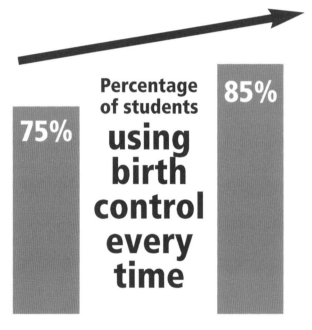

75%

Percentage of students **using birth control every time**

85%

1990s vs. today

Birth control of choice?

Those college men and women who said they had sexual intercourse in the past three months were asked, "What method(s) of birth control did you or your partner use?" (Check all that apply.)

The most popular methods of birth control used by college students are:

**the
Pill
70%**

**the
condom
57%**

Other methods, such as spermicides, diaphragm, IUD or fertility awareness, are little used **(11%).**

In fact, a third of college students (35%) report going "Double Dutch," meaning she was using the Pill as protection from pregnancy while he was using the condom as protection from sexually transmitted infections.

Results over 25 years:

It is encouraging to see that the number of **students using the Pill, condoms and Double Dutch increased over the past quarter century.** Specifically, Pill use increased from 75% in the early 1990s to 85% today. Condom use increased from approximately 45% in the 1990s to about 55% beginning in 2000 through today. Double Dutch increased from 25% in the early 1990s to 40% today.

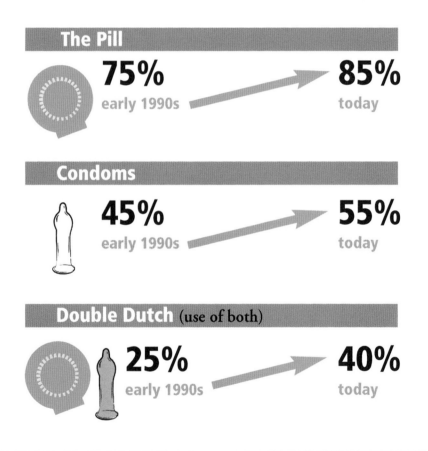

The Pill

75%
early 1990s

85%
today

Condoms

45%
early 1990s

55%
today

Double Dutch (use of both)

25%
early 1990s

40%
today

How many people have you been with?

Answers ranged from 0–25 or more sexual partners when college men and women were asked, "How many sexual partners have you had in your lifetime?"

We hear a lot about "hooking up" and "friends with benefits," creating an image of college life involving a different sexual partner every weekend. However, the average number of sex partners for college students is 3 to 4 partners. Yes, a third of college students say they have had five or more partners, but another third have had just 1 or 2 sexual partners.

the average number
of sex partners for college students is

3 to 4

Few students (11%) indicate that they have never had a sexual partner, while the majority of students (89%) have had at least one.

Upperclass students report more sexual partners than underclass students.

(Note: "Sexual partners" is not necessarily limited to sexual intercourse.)

Results over 25 years:

It may come as a surprise to learn that over the 25-year span of this study, **the incidence of having five or more partners has remained largely unchanged.** That's right. While today's college students may think having multiple partners is unique to their generation with their use of terms like "hooking up" and "friends with benefits," just as many college students 25 years ago were having multiple partners. But back then, it was called "casual sex."

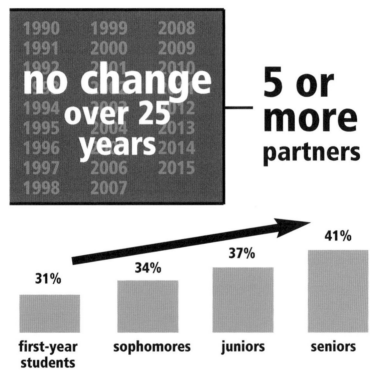

Upperclass students report 5 or more sexual partners than underclass students.

How do you feel about the number of people you've been with?

College men and women were asked, "How do you feel about the number of sex partners you have had?" Students could indicate if they felt they have had more, average or fewer partners than most people.

:(**Most college students think everybody's having more sex than they are**

— even those who are having the "average" of 3 to 4 partners, as found in this sample.

So while most (55%) think they have had fewer partners, a small percent (11%) actually feel they have had more partners than most people.

Only about a third (34%) feel they have had an average number of sexual partners. What's interesting to consider is that most of those students (62%) had actually had more than the "3 to 4 partners" average found in this sample — they had 5, 10 or even 20 or more partners. Perhaps this is a way for these students to justify a higher than average number of partners. Or maybe it's because they are in the dark about what their peers are doing, so they are left to guess how they compare to others.

Results over 25 years:

Looking over the past quarter century, it has been more common for students to feel that **all their friends are seeing more action than they are.**

55% think they have had fewer partners, a small percent (11%) actually feel they have had more partners than most people.

Ever lied about how many people you've been with?

76% tell the truth

College men and women were asked, "If a woman asked you how many sex partners you have had, would you tell her: A number higher than you've really had? A number lower than you've really had? Or the correct number?" They also were asked how they would respond if a man asked them and if their best friend asked them.

Most of the students (76%) say that they would tell the truth about how many sex partners they have had, no matter who asks them — a woman, a man or their best friend.

However, one in four (24%) would not tell the correct number (i.e., they would lie).

We see hints of the double standard in those who would lie. Most women say they'd tell a lower number of sex partners when asked by a man or a woman. Men say they would say a lower number when talking to women, but say a higher number when talking to other men.

On a more concerning note, the more partners a student says they've had, the more likely they say they would lie about it. For example, 41% of college students with five or more partners lied and 56% of those with 10 or more partners lied. The take-home message is not to rely on asking someone how many sex partners they have had. You cannot expect an honest answer, especially from those who have had many partners.

Results over 25 years:

Looking across the past quarter century, the proportion of **students who lie about the number of sexual partners they had** remains largely the same.

Ever faked it?

College men and women who have had sexual intercourse were asked, "Have you ever faked an orgasm?

Faking an orgasm is extremely common, especially for women.

Of the 4,685 respondents who say they have had intercourse, more than half (57%) indicated they have faked an orgasm. They say they aren't just doing it — they are performing it. It reflects the difference between what is really happening for them in sex and what they think should be happening.

Many more college women (70%) say they have faked an orgasm. And while the idea that women fake orgasm may be understandable to some, the idea that men can fake may seem impossible to many.

However, 28% of college men report they have faked an orgasm.

Results over 25 years:

Whether to avoid hurting their partners' feelings, build up their partners' egos or reinforce that there is nothing wrong with them, an alarming number of students have turned to faking in the past 25 years.

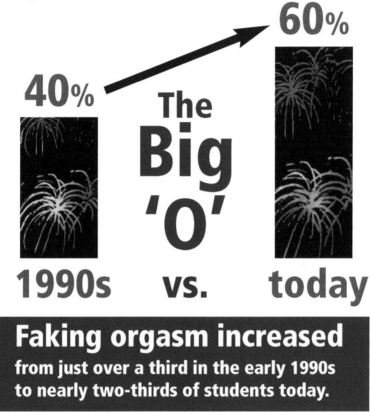

40%

60%

The Big 'O'

1990s   vs.   today

Faking orgasm increased
from just over a third in the early 1990s
to nearly two-thirds of students today.

Most of the rise can be attributed to women's behavior. For college women, faking behavior has increased dramatically over time – from less than half to nearly three-quarters of college women today saying they have faked an orgasm.

Ever masturbated?

College men and women were asked, Have you had ever masturbated?

Three-quarters (77%) of the 5,563 college students say they have masturbated. Not surprising, most of those who say they masturbate are men.

Yes

77%

of all students

Of those who have not masturbated, the majority are college women:

31% women

5% men

In fact, one-third of college women say they have never masturbated as compared to a fraction of college men (31% vs. 5%).

As women progress through college and gain a greater understanding of their body and their sexual response, as well as greater sexual experience, more women report they have masturbated (increasing from 61% of first-year women to 75% of seniors).

Results over 25 years:

Looking across the 25 years, there has been an increase in the number of college students who say they have masturbated. Since most men masturbate, the increase is due to the great numbers of women who say they pleasure themselves — from about 60% in the early 1990s to nearly 75% today.

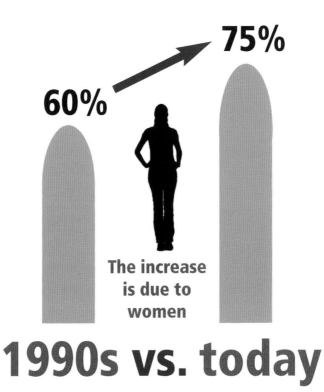

75%

60%

The increase
is due to
women

1990s vs. today

Acknowledgement of this increase in women's masturbation can be seen in the popularity of such factors as sex toy parties on college campuses.

How old were you when you started masturbating?

College students were asked, How old were you when you started masturbating?

Of the 4,305 respondents who said they masturbate, most college students (78%) say they have masturbated by the age of 16.

College men and women differ in terms of when they started masturbating.

Men indicate a much younger age for first masturbation (average age of 13), while women report a more even distribution for their age of first masturbation (ranging from 11 or younger to 19 and older). Three-quarters of college men (75%) say they started masturbating by the age of 14, while less than half of the college women have (45%).

Average age Men	Average age Women
13	11,12,13,14,15, 16,17,18,19

Results over 25 years:

Looking across the past quarter century, the average age of first masturbation has declined. However, this trend is attributed to more girls saying they first masturbated in their later teenage years (e.g., 15 to 18 years old); it is not among those who were 14 or younger.

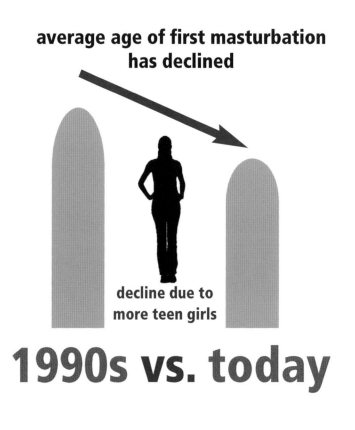

average age of first masturbation has declined

decline due to more teen girls

1990s vs. today

How often do you masturbate?

College students were asked, "Do you masturbate now?" and then asked to indicate how often. Response options ranged from "A few times in my whole life" to "More than once a day."

College men are much more likely to indicate they masturbate once a week or more compared to college women (65% of men vs.21% of women).

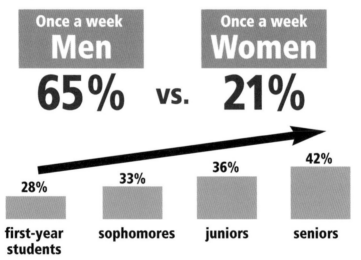

The proportion of college students reporting they masturbate once a week or more increases with class standing.

Results over 25 years:

Today, more so than in the past 25 years, there are more college men and women who report masturbating once a week or more—from less than 30% in the early 1990s to more thn 40% today.

There is an increase in masturbation for

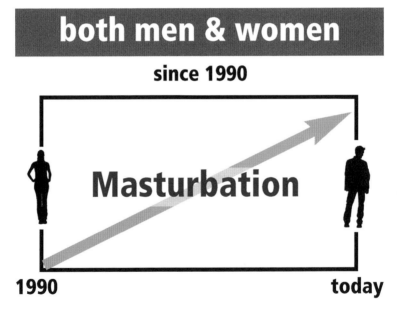

Ever had sexual experiences with someone of the same sex?

Students were asked, "Where do you see yourself along Kinsey's sexual behavior rating scale?"
Options ranged from 0 = Exclusively Heterosexual Experience to 6 = Exclusively Homosexual Experience.

The infamous "Kinsey Scale," developed back in the mid-20th century by pioneer sex researcher Alfred Kinsey, acknowledges that sexual behaviors can range from "0 = Exclusively heterosexual" to "6 = Exclusively homosexual" and offers a way to examine same-sex experiences.

83%

Have not had a same-sex experience

While the majority of college students (83%) consider themselves exclusively heterosexual (0 on the Kinsey Scale), 17% do not.

In fact, women are more likely than men (16% vs. 6%) to say they consider themselves a 1 on the Kinsey Scale, meaning heterosexual with an incidence of same-sex behavior.

Results over 25 years:

Looking over the past quarter century, **there has been a significant increase** in the number of college students who indicated they are a "1" on the Kinsey Scale (heterosexual with an incidence of same-sex experience). This is especially true for college women. Since the time of the kiss between Madonna and Brittany Spears at the MTV Video Music Awards in 2003, there's been a significant rise in the percentage of women who consider themselves a 1. A significant increase occurred from the early '90s, when only 3% of women identified themselves as heterosexual with a same-sex experience to as high as 23% today saying they have had a same-sex encounter. Whether it is making out with a girlfriend for their boyfriend's pleasure, or simply same-sex experimentation as part of normal sexual development, it is interesting to see that most of these women do not consider themselves bisexual (a 2, 3 or 4 on the Kinsey Scale).

There's been a significant rise in the percentage of women who consider themselves a '1' on the Kinsey Scale.

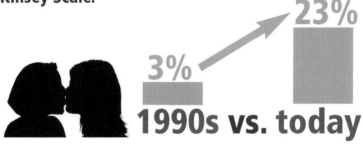

3% → 23%

1990s vs. today

Sexual Attitudes:

1990–2015 Data

1. Abstinence until marriage? Say what?

2. Is virginity important to anyone anymore?

3. Do you like oral sex?

4. Thoughts about anal sex?

5. What's love got to do with it?

6. How comfortable are you having a gay friend?

7. What are your feelings about abortion?

Abstinence until marriage? Say what?

College men and women were asked their opinion about the acceptability of premarital sex and given three options:

- "It's all right for everyone, including myself."

- "I'm against it for myself, but what others do is their business."

- "It's morally wrong for everyone."

93%
acceptable for everyone

The overwhelming majority of college students (93%) feel premarital sex is acceptable for everyone.

5%
acceptable for others

Only a small percentage feel it is not okay for themselves, but acceptable for others (5%), and even fewer (2%) think it is wrong for everyone.

2%
wrong for everyone

There was no difference between the acceptance of college men and women on this issue.

Results over 25 years:

College students' acceptance of premarital sex has remained high and unchanged over the past quarter century despite the rise in funding for abstinence-only-until-marriage programs.

No change over the past quarter century

premarital sex is accepted by an overwhelming majority

That is a 180-degree turn from how their grandparents' generation viewed premarital sex.

Is virginity important to anyone anymore?

College students were asked about their thoughts on virginity when considering a life partner (both their own and their prospective partner's virginity status) and given several options.

They were asked to indicate if they were a virgin, and then asked to choose:

"I plan to choose a life partner who is a virgin"

or

"I plan to choose a life partner who is not a virgin,"

or

"Whether my prospective partner is a virgin or not is irrelevant."

The majority

79%

of the college students surveyed felt that whether their partner is a virgin is **irrelevant** when choosing a life partner.

There was no difference between college men and women who reported that a prospective partner's virginity is irrelevant (81% vs. 79%).

However, remnants of the double standard still exist **when we look at those who say their partner's virginity status matters.**

More men want a virgin

IF virginity status matters

More women want a non-virgin

College women (17%) are much more likely than college men (11%) to say they want a sexually experienced (nonvirgin) life partner. Correspondingly, college men (8%) are much more likely than women (4%) to indicate they want a life partner who is a virgin.

Results over 25 years:

Since 1990, there has been a decline in the proportion of college students indicating that virginity is irrelevant in choosing a life partner. This is primarily due to an increase over the past 25 years in the proportion of women who indicate a preference for a life partner who is not a virgin. More women today say they want their partner to be sexually experienced.

Do you like oral sex?

College men and women were asked, "What are your personal feelings about oral sex?" Options ranged from "I think it is totally acceptable" to "I think it is wrong and should be illegal."

Yes?  No?

Of 5,578 college students who responded, nearly everyone indicated oral sex is totally acceptable **92%**

Granted, these days, most don't even consider it "real sex."

Nearly every college man (98%) indicated oral sex is totally acceptable, while fewer college women say they feel this way (89%).

The proportion of college students who say they feel oral sex is totally acceptable increased by class standing. In other words, the longer they are in college, the more likely students feel oral sex is totally acceptable — from 90% of first-year students to 95% of seniors.

Results over 25 years:

Looking across the 25 years, acceptance of oral sex has remained high, just as we know from the literature that such behavior has become commonplace over the past few decades.

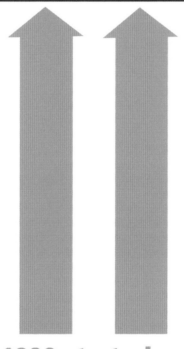

Thoughts about anal sex?

College men and women were asked, "What are your personal feelings about anal sex?"

Options ranged from

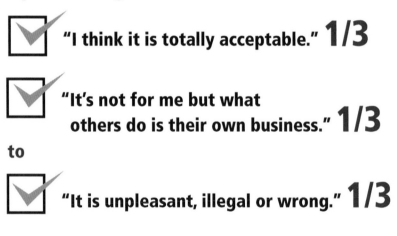

☑ "I think it is totally acceptable." **1/3**

☑ "It's not for me but what others do is their own business." **1/3**

to

☑ "It is unpleasant, illegal or wrong." **1/3**

Despite all the hype in pornography that portrays anal sex as something that is incredibly popular, only a third (34%) of the 5,576 college students say anal sex is totally acceptable. Whether it's to please a partner, try something new, avoid pregnancy or maintain one's virginity, few college students rate anal sex as acceptable.

Another one-third (31%) say that while they personally find it unacceptable, what others do is their own business. The final one-third indicates that they either find the while idea unpleasant (18%) or feel anal sex is disgusting (16%). Very few feel anal sex is wrong and should be illegal (1%).

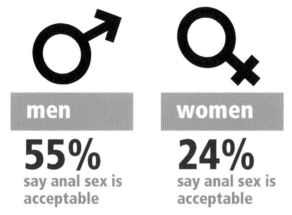

men

55%
say anal sex is
acceptable

women

24%
say anal sex is
acceptable

When comparing their thoughts on anal sex, more than half of college men (55%) feel anal sex is totally acceptable, while only a quarter (24%) of college women feel this way. It is no surprise that so few women rate it high, considering how many women report it is uncomfortable or downright painful.

Upperclass students are more accepting of anal sex. Overall, only 29% of first-year students think it's totally fine, whereas 40% of seniors do.

Results over 25 years:

Anal sex has become more acceptable, especially to men. While only one-third felt anal sex was totally acceptable in the early 1990s, today over three-quarters of men feel this way.

What's love got to do with it?

College students were asked, "How important is it for you to be in love with the person you are having sex with?"

Response options ranged from "very important" to "unimportant."

For most people, love and sex are closely linked. That is, unless you're a college student.

Of the 5,580 college students who answered this question, just 59% of college students say being in love is important. The term "making love" is less likely to be used by today's college students to describe this activity.

College students responded:

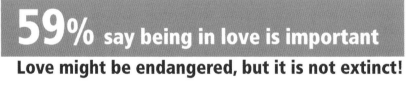

59% say being in love is important

Love might be endangered, but it is not extinct!

The differences in responses by college women and men reveal that when it comes to some things with sex, the double standard is alive and well. Many more college women (67%) feel love is important in a sexual relationship, whereas far fewer college men (43%) feel the same way. Conversely, a quarter of college men (26%) say being in love is not important when it comes to sex (and perhaps not even knowing his partner's name?), whereas only 11% of women say this. For many college students today (men especially), sex is not seen as something special you do with someone special.

Results over 25 years:

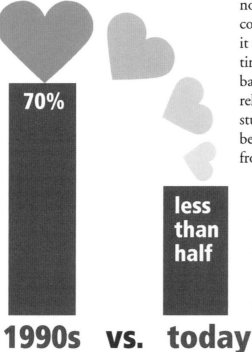

70%

less than half

1990s vs. today

From about 70% in the early 1990s to now less than half of college students seeing it as important. Over time, love has taken a backseat in the sexual relationships of college students. Sex has become detached from love.

In the past 25 years, being in love as an important component of sex has fallen sharply

How comfortable are you having a gay friend?

College students were asked about their level of comfort with having a gay friend. They were asked to consider a situation in which they discover their best friend is gay when she/he reveals the desire to have a sexual experience. Response options to measure level of comfort included: "One of distress. I would terminate the relationship," "I would refuse the invite and say that our friendship depends on the homosexuality being kept private," and "I would refuse the invitation, but say that their homosexuality would not affect our friendship."

83% are accepting of their gay friends

For the 4,609 students who consider themselves exclusively heterosexual, most (83%) indicate they were accepting of their gay friend and this would not affect their relationship.

Many more women (90%) than men (68%) indicate their acceptance and that this would not affect their relationship. In contrast, one out of five (21%) of the college men say they would want to terminate the relationship, while few (6%) of the women would do so.

Results over 25 years:

Looking across the 25 years, there has been a dramatic increase in the proportion of students who report that they are accepting of a gay friend, **increasing from 60% in the early 1990s to 90% today.**

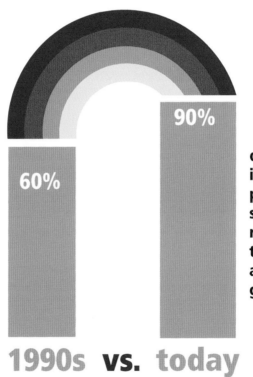

90%

60%

dramatic increase in the proportion of students who report that they are accepting of a gay friend

1990s **vs.** today

What are your feelings about abortion?

College men and women were asked about their feelings on abortion. Specifically, students were asked how supportive they are of the Supreme Court decision, Roe v Wade, which legalized abortion. Responses ranged from "I fully agree" to "I fully disagree."

76% agree with the Roe v Wade decision

Of the 5,529 college students who answered this question, the majority (76%) of students agree with the Supreme Court decision on abortion. Some (21%) are opposed to abortion, but feel there should be exceptions made for the health of the mother and in cases of rape. Few (3%) disagree and feel it should be overturned.

In addition, the longer you are in college, the more supportive you become. While 70% of first-year students fully support Roe v Wade, 81% of seniors fully support this Supreme Court decision.

Results over 25 years:

Across the quarter century, most college students continue to fully support a woman's right to choose.

However, there has been a decline in full support of Roe v Wade in the past 25 years, as an increasing number of students say it should be allowed only in certain circumstances, such as when a mother's life is in danger or in the case of rape. Full support of Roe v Wade went from a high of 85% in the early 1990s to 75% in more recent years.

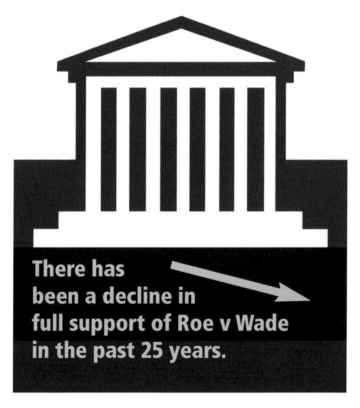

There has been a decline in full support of Roe v Wade in the past 25 years.

Parental Influence:

1990–2015 Data

1. What would mom say if she knew?

2. What would dad say if he knew?

3. Ever asked mom a question about sex?

4. Ever asked dad a question about sex?

5. Did your parents influence your views on sex?

What would mom say if she knew?

College students were asked, "What is your mother's feelings about your having premarital sex?" Options were "She would be opposed," "She would not mind if we were in love" or "She would be in favor of it." Students were also given the option "I don't know."

74% think mom would say:

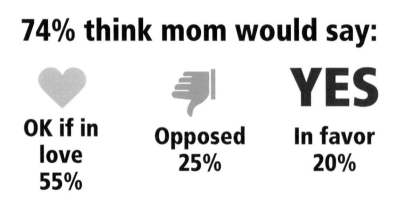

OK if in love 55%

Opposed 25%

In favor 20%

26% don't know what mom would say.

Of the 5,589 college student respondents, one-quarter (26%) of students say they don't know what mom's feelings are. Of the 4,113 who expressed an opinion, more than half (55%) feel she would not mind if they were in love. For mom, love should have something to do with it. However, a quarter (25%) think she would be opposed. Fewer (20%) believe their mother would be in favor.

College women are more likely than college men to think their mother would be okay as long as they are in love (57% vs. 50%). On the other hand, many more college men than women feel their mother would be in favor of them having premarital sex (28% of the men vs. only 17% of the women).

Results over 25 years:

There has been an increase over time in the proportion of students (mostly women) who think their mother is okay with their premarital sex, especially if they are in love (from 50% to 60% today). There has also been an increase in college students believing that their mom would be in favor of them having sex (from 15% to 25% today).

50% **60%**

1990s vs. today
More students today think mom would be OK with premarital sex if they were in love.

What would dad say if he knew?

College students were asked, "What is your father's feelings about your having premarital sex?" Options were "He would be opposed," "He would not mind if we were in love" or "He would be in favor of it." Students were also given the option, "I don't know."

59% think dad would say:

YES

OK if in love 40%

Opposed 37%

In favor 23%

41% don't know what dad would say.

Of the 5,586 college students who answered this question, many (41%) did not know their father's opinion. Of the 3,278 who had an opinion about their dad's perspective, 40% say dad would be opposed, and nearly as many (37%) feel he would be okay if love was involved. Fewer (23%) believe he would be in favor.

Remnants of the double standard are reflected in the student responses about their dad. **College women are much more likely than college men to report their father is opposed to her having premarital sex (46% vs. 17%).** In contrast, men are much more likely than women (47% vs. 11%) to report their father is in favor of him having premarital sex. Women are more likely than men to report their father would not mind if they were in love (43% and 36%).

Results over 25 years:

Across time, there has been an increase in students who think their father is in favor (from 20% to nearly 30% today). This increase is due to the many men who feel their father is in favor (from 40% in the early 1990s to over 60% today).

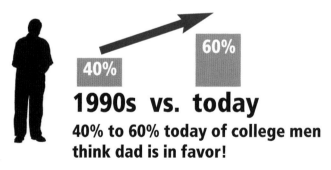

1990s vs. today
40% to 60% today of college men think dad is in favor!

Ever asked mom a question about sex?

College students were asked, "How often did you ask your mother questions about sexuality before you came to college?" Response options ranged from "Never' to "Very frequently."

A little over half have asked mom a question or two

35%
never asked mom a sex question

Of the 5,579 college students who answered this question, about one-third (35%) report they have never asked their mother a question related to sex. A little over half (54%) have at least asked a question or two. Few (11%) indicated that they have often or frequently asked their mom questions about sex.

54%
asked mom one or two questions

11%
asked mom frequent sex questions

College women (70%) are much more likely than college men (53%) to report they have asked their mother a question.

Results over 25 years:

Despite years of advocating the importance of parents as sexual educators of their children, there has been very little change.

Across the 25 years, the proportion of students who report they have asked their mother questions about sex has remained static.

Ever asked dad a question about sex?

College students were asked, "How often did you ask your father questions about sexuality before you came to college? Response options ranged from "Never' to "Very frequently."

Dad is nearly nonexistent in conversations about sex.

75% never asked dad a sex question

22% asked dad one or two questions

3% asked dad frequent sex questions

Dad is nearly nonexistent in the conversations about sex. Of the 5,583 college students who answered this question, the majority (75%) report they have never asked their father a single question about sex. However, almost a quarter (22%), say they have at least approached dad with a question about sex once or twice. Barely 3% say they often turn to dad for answers to sex questions.

What's a blow job?

Do I need
contraception?

For those few students (25%) who report they have asked
their father a question, men (42%) are much more likely than
women (18%) to report they have done so.

Results over 25 years:

Across the quarter century,

there has been
very little
change.
in the proportion of
students who say
they have asked their
father questions
about sex. Most college
students do not turn to
their father for answers
about sex-related issues.

DAD

Did your parents influence your views on sex?

College students were asked, "Which has been your most important source of influence on your sexuality?" Options: mother, father, both parents equally, siblings of the same sex, siblings of the other sex, friends of the same sex, friends of the other sex, religion, media or school.

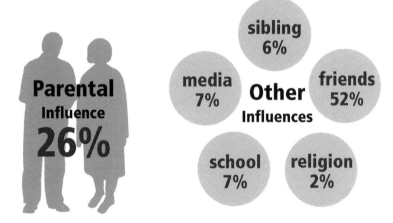

Only one-quarter (26%) report that their parents (mother, father or both parents equally) are the most important source of influence on their sexuality. The majority of students say their friends (52%) are the most important influence on their sexual attitudes, particularly same-sex friends (42%).

Other influencers identified less frequently were media (7%), school (7%), siblings (6%) and religion (2%).

Results over 25 years:

Across the years, friends are identified as the most important influence on college students' sexual attitudes, especially same-sex friends.

Friends have the most influence on sexual attitudes.

For most students, parents are not seen as influencing their sex lives.

Safer Sex
and HIV/AIDS:

1990–2015
Data

1. How concerned are you about HIV/AIDS?

2. Has your behavior changed in response to HIV/AIDS?

How likely are you to…..

- Ask how many sex partners the person has had?
- Try to guess if a partner might be HIV+?
- Take fewer precautions if a partner does not seem like type?
- Ask for a monogamous relationship?
- Ask a partner if she/he has been tested for HIV?
- Have both of you tested for HIV?
- Discuss using a condom before sex?
- Refuse sex without a condom?

How concerned are you about HIV?

College men and women were asked, "How concerned are you that HIV/AIDS will spread widely among the nation's college students/young adults?" Response options: very concerned, somewhat concerned, not at all concerned, uncertain

54% very concerned — Women

45% very concerned — Men

Of the 5,585 college students who answered this question, the overwhelming majority (90%) express concern about HIV/AIDS. Specifically, 51% are very concerned and 39% somewhat concerned.

College women are more likely than men to report they are "very concerned" (54% vs. 45%) that HIV will spread.

Results over 25 years:

However, over the past quarter century, the level of concern surrounding HIV/AIDS has decreased dramatically. Fewer students are "very concerned" today compared to 25 years ago. The further we have moved from the time when HIV first became an issue in the 1980s and was seen by many as a death sentence, the less concern there is. This change is seen in the 1990s, perhaps with the introduction of better treatment that changed the face of AIDS to a long-term, manageable illness. While more than three-quarters of college students were very concerned in the 1990s, less than one-quarter (22%) of students today indicate they are very concerned. In addition, very few (less than 1%) were unconcerned in the 1990s, whereas today almost 20% of college students say they are not concerned at all about HIV/AIDS.

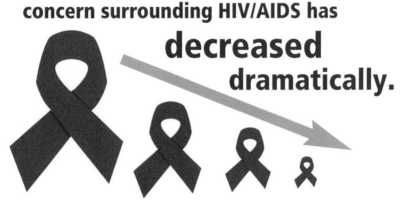

Over 25 years, the level of concern surrounding HIV/AIDS has **decreased dramatically.**

Has your behavior changed in response to HIV?

College students were asked, "Has your behavior changed in response to the HIV/AIDS epidemic?" and given the response options of either Yes or No.

Both men and women responded

No.

Of the 5,515 college students who answered this question, two-thirds (63%) report they have not changed their behavior in response to HIV/AIDS.

There was no difference in the proportion of college men and women who report they changed their behavior in response to the HIV/AIDS epidemic.

In terms of class standing, the longer they are in college, the more likely they are to say they have changed their behavior in response to HIV.

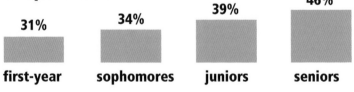

| 31% | 34% | 39% | 46% |
| first-year | sophomores | juniors | seniors |

Results over 25 years:

In the past 25 years, there has been a
significant decrease
in the proportion of students who report that
they have changed their behavior, from 60% of
students in the 1990s to 20% today. For many of
today's college students, the AIDS epidemic is perceived as a
distant memory and therefore a decreasing number of college
students don't see an urgency to change their behavior. For
others, HIV has been a reality for their generation, resulting
in safe sex practices. They are not changing their behavior
because they are already practicing safer sex.

I changed my behavior

60%   20%

1990s vs. today

How likely are you to... ask how many sex partners the person has had?

A majority (81%) of students indicate they were likely to ask a potential sex partner how many partners he or she has had.

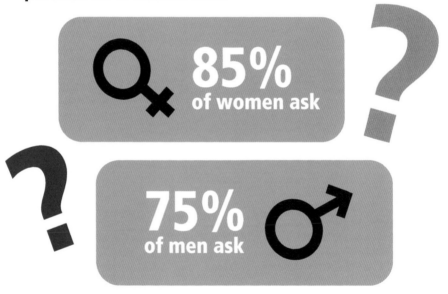

85%
of women ask

75%
of men ask

Women were more likely than men (85% of women vs. 75% of men) to say they would ask a potential partner about the number of previous partners.

Results over 25 years:

Despite an increase in the late 1990s in the number of college students who said they would ask about previous sex partners (90% would ask), college students today are just as likely as they were 25 years ago to ask how many previous sex partners a person has had (70% in the early 1990s and today).

College students today are
just as likely
to ask how many previous partners...

...you're sleeping with everyone your partner has slept with :(

How likely are you to... try to guess if a partner might be HIV+?

A majority (58%) of students indicate they are likely to guess if their partner might be HIV+. And men and women are equally likely to try to guess if their potential partner is HIV+.

58%
of men and women
are likely to guess

Results over 25 years:

As we look over time, today's college students are much less likely to try to guess if their partner might be HIV+ as compared to those in the early 1990s, from 70% back then to 45% today.

likely to guess HIV+

70% **45%**

1990s vs. today

How likely are you to... take fewer precautions if a partner does not seem like the type?

Less than half (45%) of college students say they'd take fewer precautions if a partner does not seem like the type to be infected.

Men were more likely than women to say they would take fewer precautions if their potential sex partner does not seem like the type to be infected. Men were more likely than women to be risk takers and forgo such things as using a condom if the person does not seem like the type. (52% of men vs. only 42% of women.)

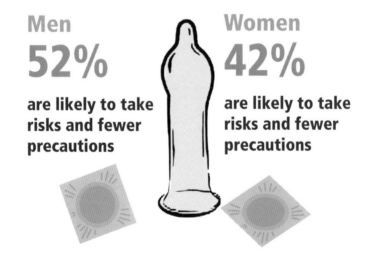

Men
52%
are likely to take risks and fewer precautions

Women
42%
are likely to take risks and fewer precautions

Results over 25 years:

From the early 1990s to 2000, the percentage of students who say they are likely to take

fewer precautions dropped from 60% to about 30%.

However, since 2000, there has been an increase in risk-taking, with nearly half of college students saying they are likely to take fewer precautions if a potential sex partner does not seem like the type to be infected.

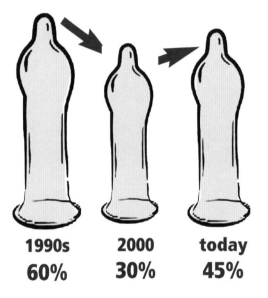

1990s	2000	today
60%	30%	45%

likely to take fewer precautions

How likely are you to... ask for a monogamous relationship?

A majority (76%) of students indicated they are likely to ask to have a monogamous relationship.
Women are more likely than men to say they are likely to ask to have a monogamous relationship (81% of women vs. 66% of men).

ask to be
Monogamous
76%

Women **81%** ask for a monogamous relationship

Men **66%** ask for a monogamous relationship

Results over 25 years:

When examining trends over 25 years, there was an increase from the early 1990s to 2000 **in college students' likelihood of asking their partner for a monogamous relationship (from about 75% to 85%).** However, in the past 15 years, fewer students say they are likely to do this — only about 55%

Let's only date each other

I want to be the only one!

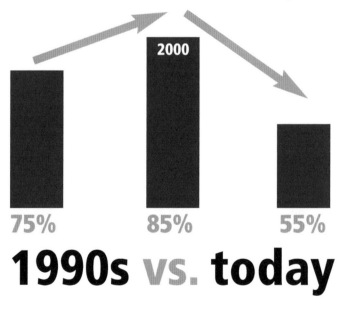

2000

75%   85%   55%

1990s vs. today

How likely are you to... ask a partner if she/he has been tested for HIV?

Half (50%) of college students say they are likely to ask their potential sex partners if they have been tested.

Women are more likely than men to say they will ask their sex partners if they have been tested (54% vs. 39%)

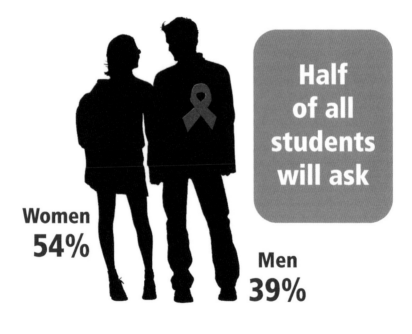

Women 54%

Half of all students will ask

Men 39%

Results over 25 years:

Over time, attitudes toward testing have changed greatly.

In the early 1990s only 20% of college students were likely to ask their partner about being tested, but by the late 1990s, 70% were likely to do this. However, since 2000, less than half of college students say they are likely to inquire about if their partner has had an HIV antibody test.

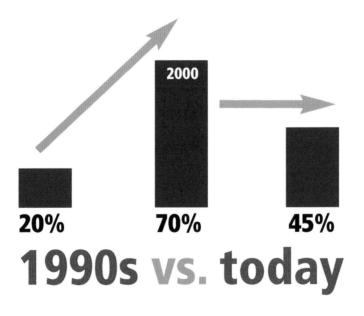

1990s vs. today

How likely are you to... have both of you tested for HIV?

A minority of college students (36%) indicated they are likely to have both of them tested for HIV antibodies.

College women were much more likely than college men to say they would have both of them tested for HIV antibodies (39% of women and 28% of men).

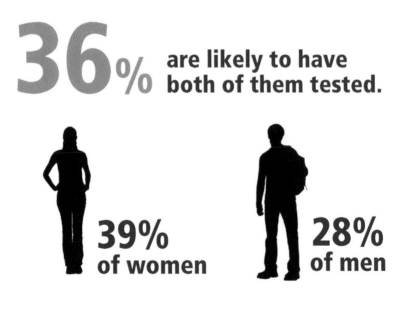

36% are likely to have both of them tested.

39% of women

28% of men

Results over 25 years:

In terms of change over time,

the first half of the 1990s saw
an increase in the likelihood of having both
people tested (from 11% to 50% by 1995).

However, after 1995, this likelihood declined.

Fewer college students say they would insist that both they
and their partner be tested. Since 1996, only about a third
(32%) say they are likely to have both of them be tested for
HIV antibodies.

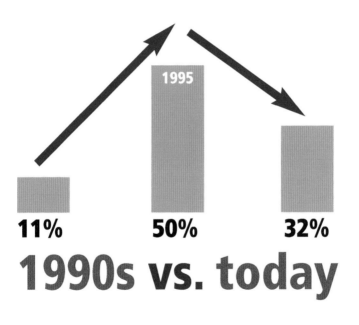

11%   50%   32%

1990s vs. today

How likely are you to... discuss using a condom before sex?

A majority (90%) of students indicate they are likely to discuss using a condom before having sex.

Women are more likely than men to say they will discuss using a condom with a potential partner (91% of women vs. 85% of men).

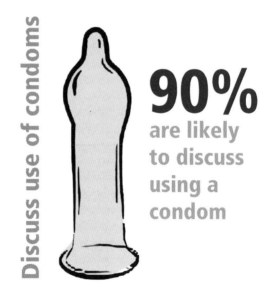

Discuss use of condoms

90%
are likely
to discuss
using a
condom

Results over 25 years:

Although the likelihood of discussing condom use with a partner has remained high across the 25 years (90% or higher), there has been a slow steady decline.

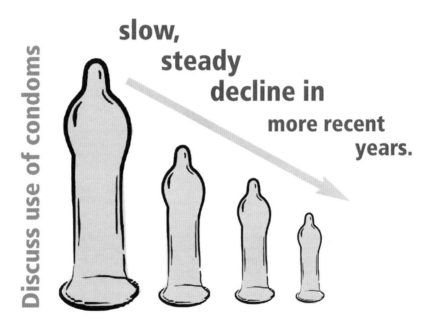

How likely are you to... refuse sex without a condom?

A majority (77%) of students indicated they are likely to refuse sexual activity without a condom.

Women are more likely than men to say they will refuse sex without a condom (84% vs. 61%).

77% No condom, no sex.

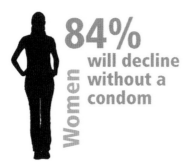
84%
will decline
without a
condom

Women

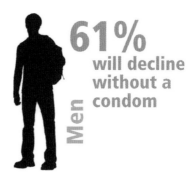
61%
will decline
without a
condom

Men

Results over 25 years:

Looking across the past quarter century, there was an increase in the number of students who said they would refuse sex without a condom **in the early 1990s.** This increase remained high through 2005. **However, since that time, there has been a decline, with fewer college students today saying they would be likely to refuse sex without a condom — the same as in the early 1990s (65%).**

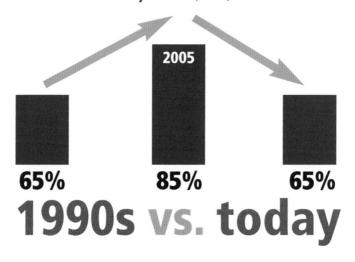

2005

65%   85%   65%

1990s vs. today

Difficult Side
of Sexuality:

1990–2015 Data

1. Do you know anyone who has had an STI?

2. Ever had an STI?

3. Know anyone who has had an abortion?

4. Ever been involved in a pregnancy that ended in abortion?

5. Do you know anyone who has been raped?

6. Have you ever been raped?

7. Ever had an involuntary sexual experience?

8. Were you sexually abused as a child?

Do you know anyone who has had an STI?

College students were asked, Do you know anyone personally who has had a sexually transmitted infection?

YES 56%

Most college students (56%) say they know someone who has had a sexually transmitted infection (STI). This should come as no surprise, since STIs and college students remain an ongoing concern.

There is no difference between college women and men who know someone with an STI (56% and 55%).

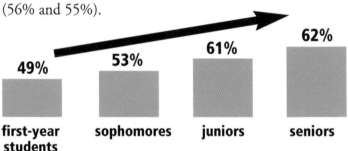

49% first-year students

53% sophomores

61% juniors

62% seniors

The longer they are in college, the more likely they are to say they personally know someone who has had a sexually transmitted infection.

Results over 25 years:

Across time, the proportion of college
students who say they
know someone who has had a
STI has decreased.

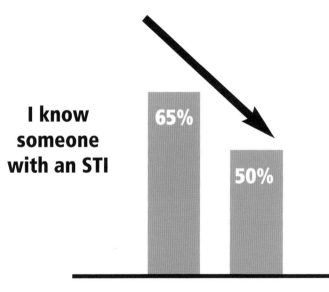

I know
someone
with an STI

65%

50%

1990s vs. today

Ever had an STI?

College students were asked, "Have you ever had a sexually transmitted infection (STI)?"

Nine percent (n=405) of sexually active college men and women say they have had a sexually transmitted infection.

women   men

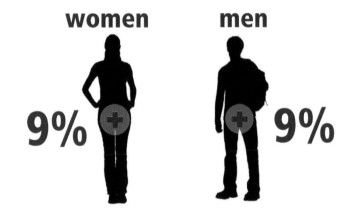

9%   9%

There was no difference between college men and women.

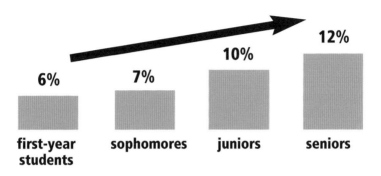

6%	7%	10%	12%
first-year students	sophomores	juniors	seniors

In terms of class standing, the longer students have been in college, the more likely they are to say that they have had an STI.

Results over 25 years:

Across time, the proportion of college students who report having an STI has decreased, from a high of 20% in the early 1990s to a low of 5% today, reflecting greater safer sex practices by these students in recent years.

Know anyone who has had an abortion?

College students were asked, "Do you know anyone personally who has had an abortion?"

62%
know someone who has.

Two-thirds of college student (62%) reported that they knew someone who has had an abortion.

Women (66%) were much more likely than men (52%) to know someone personally who has had an abortion.

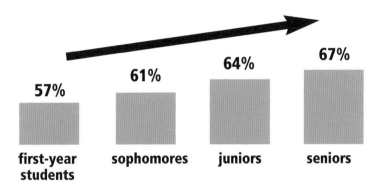

57% first-year students
61% sophomores
64% juniors
67% seniors

The longer students have been in college, the more likely they are to say that they know someone personally who has had an abortion (57% first-year students to 67% of seniors).

Results over 25 years:

75%

50%

With fewer unplanned pregnancies across the past quarter century, the proportion of students who reported they know someone personally who has had an abortion has also decreased — from 75% in the early 1990s to 50% today.

Ever been involved in a pregnancy that ended in abortion?

College students were asked, "Have you been involved in a pregnancy that ended in abortion?"

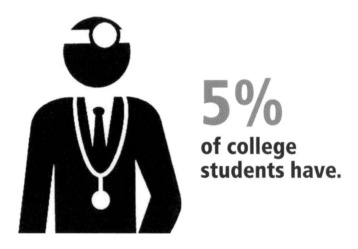

5%
of college students have.

Of the 4,796 respondents, few (5%) college students report that they had been involved in a pregnancy that ended in abortion.

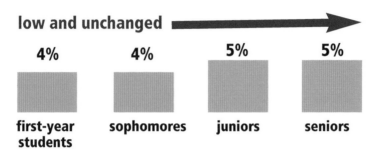

low and unchanged ➔

4%	4%	5%	5%
first-year students	sophomores	juniors	seniors

There is no difference between college women and men who had experienced this and no difference by class standing.

Results over 25 years:

Across time, the proportion of college students who report they been involved with a pregnancy that ended in an abortion remained low and actually decreased over the 25 years.

Do you know anyone who has been raped?

College students were asked, "Do you know anyone personally who has been raped?"

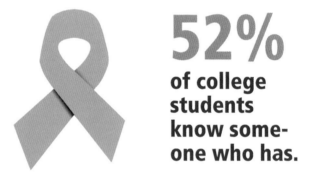

52%
of college students know some-one who has.

Slightly more than half of college students (52%) know someone personally who has been raped. Women are more likely than men to know someone (54% vs. 48%)

The proportion of college women who report they know someone personally who had been raped increased the longer they had been in college, from half (50%) of first-year women to 60% of senior women knowing someone who had been raped.

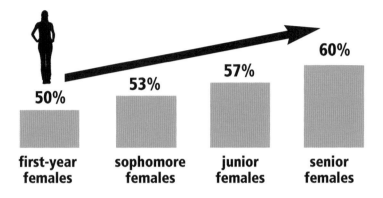

50% first-year females
53% sophomore females
57% junior females
60% senior females

There was an increase from half (50%) of first-year women to 60% of senior women knowing someone who had been raped.

Results over 25 years:

Over 25 years, the proportion of college students who reported they know someone personally who had been raped

has remained relatively unchanged.

Have you ever been raped?

College students were asked, "Have you ever been raped?"

9% of college students report that they have experienced rape.

11% report having been raped

Women

4% report having been raped

Men

College women are more likely to say they have been raped as compared to men (11% vs. 4%)

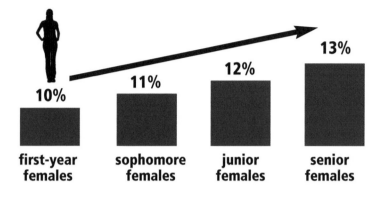

10% first-year females   11% sophomore females   12% junior females   13% senior females

In terms of class standing, the proportion of women who report they had been raped increased the longer they had been in college, from 10% of first-year women to 13% of seniors. That is one in eight college women.

Results over 25 years:

Across time, the proportion of college students who report that they have been raped

remained relatively unchanged.

Ever had an involuntary sexual experience?

College students were asked, "Have you ever been involved in an involuntary sexual experience?"

One-third (30%) of college students report having been involved in an involuntary sexual experience.

37% had an involuntary sexual experience

Women

16% had an involuntary sexual experience

Men

College women (37%) are much more likely than college men (16%) to report that they have been involved in an involuntary sexual experience.

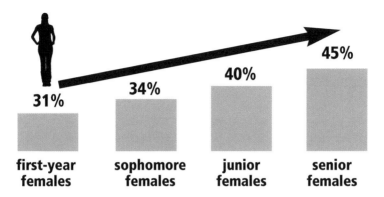

In terms of class standing, the longer students have been in college, the more likely they are to say that they have been involved in an involuntary sexual experience. It is women who are more likely to say they experienced involuntary sexual experience - increasing from a third (31%) of first-year college women to nearly half (45%) of seniors.

Results over 25 years:

Across time, the proportion of students who reported they have been involved in an involuntary sexual experience **decreased.**

Notice the discrepancy between those who said they have been raped (9%) and those who said they had experienced an involuntary sexual experience (30%). Although involuntary sexual experience refers to a broader range of behaviors, I have found that students do not usually characterize their involuntary sexual experience as rape for a number of reasons: they don't understand the definition of rape or have a sensationalized image of what "real rape" is, they don't want to categorize the person who assaulted them as a rapist, or because they blame themselves for what happened.

Were you sexually abused as a child?

College students were asked, "Would you consider yourself a victim of child sexual abuse?"

1:12
were abused as children

One in 12 (8%) college students consider themselves a victim of child sexual abuse.

College women (10%) are much more likely than college men (4%) to report that they experienced childhood sexual abuse.

Women
10%

Men
4%

Results over 25 years:

Across the past 25 years, the proportion of college students who self-identified as victims of childhood sexual abuse decreased. This is consistent with dramatic declines reported in national studies, suggesting that decades of coordinated efforts to increase awareness and prevention, along with better training of professionals and the prosecution of offenders, have brought down the rate of child sexual abuse.

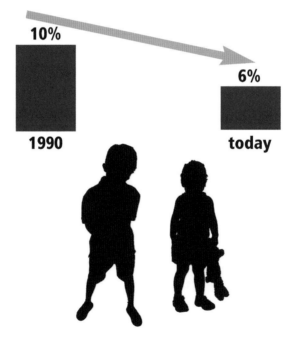

10%

6%

1990

today

Newer Data Set

2010–2015*

1. Have you used the morning-after pill?
2. Do you do a monthly self-exam?
3. Penis size? Breast size?
4. Have you ever shaved?
5. Sex without a condom?
6. What have you done sexually?
7. Technology and sex
8. Planes, trains and automobiles
9. Ever lied to get someone in bed?
10. Ever gotten someone drunk?
11. Had an intentional one-night stand?
12. Ever cheated on a partner?
13. Why are you most likely to have sex?
14. How does your sex life stack up?
15. Longest you've gone without sex?
16. Greatest age difference?
17. The adjective that best describes sex?
18. Favorite position?
19. How often do you reach orgasm?
20. Are you satisfied?

*Results are based on responses of 1,360 students

95

Have you used the morning-after pill?

College men and women were asked, "Have you ever used emergency contraception?"

For those students who reported they were sexually active, a third of respondents report they used emergency contraception, the pill taken soon after unprotected sex to prevent pregnancy.

1/3 have used the morning-after pill

Many more college women than men reported that emergency contraception was used (36% vs. 24%). Perhaps one reason for the discrepancy — he did not know she had taken it.

Do you do a monthly self-exam?

College students were asked about self-exams. Women were asked, "Do you do a regular/monthly breast self-exam? Men were asked "Do you do a regular/ monthly testicular self-exam?"

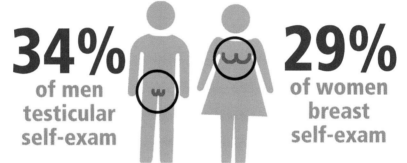

34%
of men
testicular
self-exam

29%
of women
breast
self-exam

Although the American Cancer Society recommends a monthly self-exam for early detection of breast and testicular cancers, the survey found only about a third of college students say they do this.

Only 34% of men and 29% of women report that they do self-exams. **Clearly there is more work to do on the prevention front.**

Penis size?
Breast Size?

College students were asked to rate themselves. For men: "How do you rate the size of your penis?" For women: "How do you rate the size of your breasts?" The response options: "Below average," "About Average," and "Above Average."

Half the students rated their body parts as "about average."

It should come as no surprise that there were big differences between men and women when it comes to "below average," with many more women rating their breasts this way (25%), while few men rated their penis size as below average (8%). College men do not seem to have the insecurities of penis size.

 **8%** rate their penis size below average

Men

 **25%** rate their breast size below average

Women

Have you ever shaved?

College students were asked, "Have you ever shaved your pubic area?" Response options ranged from "trim," "partial," "full," "all of the above" or "never."

98% yes

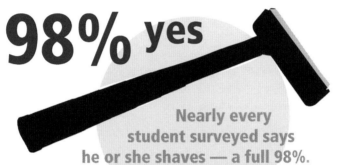

Nearly every student surveyed says he or she shaves — a full 98%.

College men are just as likely as women to say they shave their pubic region, but there appears to be variations in how much hair they remove. More women say they remove all their pubic hair (48%), while more men say they trim (23%).

Pubic hair removal is the new norm among today's college men and women. Whether it is due to the rise in skimpy bathing suits, oral sex or porn stars shaving in order to increase and enhance the view of their genitals, pubic hair shaving has become mainstream.

Sex without a condom?

College students were asked, "Since coming to college, have you had sex without a condom because...." and a range of reasons were given.

	Women	Men
I was sure that my partner was disease free.	54%	46%
I just assumed my partner was disease free.	29%	33%
I was drunk or high.	32%	31%
I didn't care.	24%	30%
I didn't want to spoil the mood.	19%	20%
I was lazy.	13%	21%

	Women	Men
My partner was too hot.	8%	18%
I was worried about my partner's response.	8%	7%
My partner refused to use a condom.	6%	9%

For many of these reasons, college men and women are similar.

However, **more men than women** say they don't use a condom because: **they don't care, they are lazy or think their partner is too hot.**

She was too hot to stop!!!

:-)

What have you done sexually?

College students were asked to check what they have done sexually from a list of options. When looking at the responses for those who are sexually active, we see that college students engage in a variety of sexual behaviors.

	Women	Men
Talked dirty	87%	89%
Included spanking	63%	70%
Used a vibrator or other sex toy by yourself*	48%	13%
Included a vibrator or other sex toy with a partner	29%	26%
Included role play in your sexual experience	27%	30%
Included bondage (e.g. you or your partner tied up)	28%	27%

*includes those who said they have masturbated

	Women	Men
Had a "friend with benefits"	64%	67%
Had a one night stand	50%	64%
Made out with someone of the same sex just because	33%	2%
Had a threesome	10%	13%
Had sex with a much older person	14%	14%

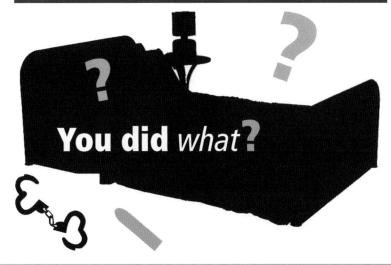

You did *what*?

Technology and sex

College students were asked, "In terms of use of technology, have you ever…" and were instructed to check off whatever they have participated in.

The Internet, social media and cell phones have given us more options than ever before when it comes to sex.

 According to these results, sexting (the sending or receiving of nude pictures) is fairly common, as is being photographed nude. Nearly all the college men say and two-thirds of the college women say they have viewed pornography online. Phone sex is still around and now is complimented by the increasing popularity of sex online.

	Women	Men
Received nude pictures of someone else?	61%	77%
Had nude pictures taken of yourself?	46%	42%
Sent nude pictures of yourself to someone?	56%	44%
Been filmed having sex?*	12%	18%
Had phone sex?*	36%	40%
Had sex online?•	31%	37%
Met someone online for sex?*	4%	12%
Viewed pornography online (pictures or video)	69%	98%
Watched an X-rated movie	53%	83%

*includes only those students who said they have had sex

Planes, trains and automobiles

College students were asked, "Where have you had sex?" and were presented with a checklist of places.

Places:

Have you ever had sex:	Total
outdoors?	63%
in a public building?	30%
in your parent's bed?	26%
at your workplace?	11%
in the library?	5%
in a nightclub/bar?	3%

College students report that sex isn't just for the bedroom. Both college men and women report similar experiences in the various venues. The most common is in a car (77%), followed by outdoors (63%). Only 2% have membership in the mile high club. A third have taken a chance by having sex in a public building, and about a quarter have had sex in their parents' bed. And as these results show, there is more going on in the library stacks than studying for 5% of college students.

Transportation:

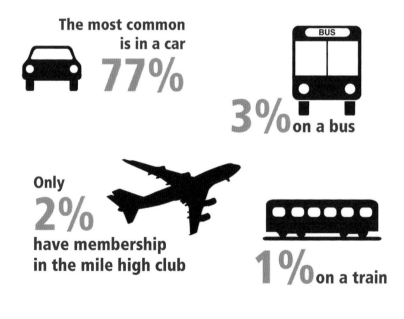

The most common is in a car
77%

BUS
3% on a bus

Only **2%** have membership in the mile high club

1% on a train

Ever lied to get someone in bed?

Students were asked, "Have you ever lied to get someone in bed?" Approximately 1 in 10 college students (9%) say they have lied in order to get someone to have sex.

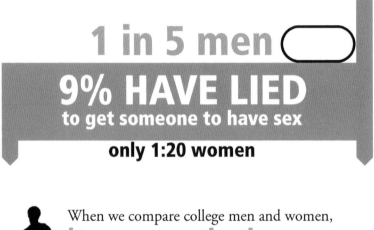

1 in 5 men

9% HAVE LIED
to get someone to have sex

only 1:20 women

When we compare college men and women, **it was mostly the men— nearly one in five (21%)** who say they have done this.
Just a heads up about the pickup lines.

Ever gotten someone drunk?

College men and women were asked, "Have you ever tried to get someone drunk or high in order to get that person into bed?" Few college students (6%) say they have tried to get someone drunk or high in order to get that person into bed.

When comparing men and women, **college men were much more likely than college women** to say they have done this (13% vs. only 4%)

Few college students say they've done this

Had an intentional one-night stand?

College students were asked, "Have you ever slept with someone knowing you would never call again?"

Approximately a third of students (30%) report sleeping with someone knowing they would never call him or her again.

Many more college men (44%) than college women (25%) say they have done this.

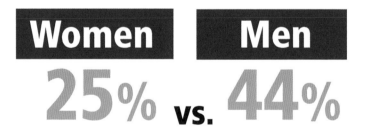

knowing they would never call him or her again

Women **Men**

25% vs. 44%

Ever cheated on a partner?

College students were asked, "Have you ever cheated on a steady partner?"

Approximately a quarter of college students (24%) say they have cheated on a steady partner. There is little difference between college men and women who say they have done this (23% of women vs. 27% of men).

1/4
have cheated

little difference in men and women

Why are you most likely to have sex?

College men and women were asked, "The reason you are most likely to have sex with someone is...."

The top two responses were **love 55%**

and
attraction 38%

College men say the reason they are most likely to have sex is because the person is attractive (60%), while women said they do it for love (62%).

The double standard endures the test of time.

Women	Men
62% say love	**60% say attractive**

How does your sex life stack up?

College students were asked, "Compared to other people your age, your sex life is..." with response options of better than most, about the same or not as good.

Less than half (40%) of college students feel their sex life is about the same as their peers. About one third (34%) feel that their sex life is better than most and a quarter (26%) feel their sex life is not as good as others.

There are no differences between men and women.

40% about the same
34% better
26% not as good

Longest you've gone without sex?

College students were asked, "Since coming to college, what is the longest you have gone without having sex?" Response options ranged from a few days, weeks, months or a year or more.

48%
have gone a few months or more without sex

Despite an image of college involving sex every weekend, nearly half (48%) of the sexually active college students say they have gone a few months or more without sex (7% of these have gone a year or more). More than a third (38%) have gone a few weeks. The rest of the college students (14%) report they have gone a few days without sex. There is no difference between college men and women on this question.

Greatest age difference?

Similar age
80%

College students were asked, "What has been the greatest age difference between you and a consensual sex partner?"

Most say their sex partners are similar in age (80%). College women are more likely to say they  have had an older partner, with nearly 20% having had a sex partner five or more years their senior. When it comes to the "cougar effect," 5% of the college men say they have had a sexual partner who is 10 or more years older.

The adjective that best describes sex?

College students were asked, "What adjective best describes your attitude toward sex?"

Most college students describe their attitude toward sex as

adventurous 40%
self-confident 31%
cautious 17%

In terms of differences between college men and women in the way they describe their attitudes toward sex, college men are more likely to say they are adventurous (47%) while college women are more likely than men to say they are cautious (20%).

Women 20%
say they are
cautious

Men 47%
say they are
adventurous

Favorite Position?

College students were asked, "What is your favorite sexual position?" and given response options: missionary or man on top, woman on top, doggie style, the spoon or not applicable/none of these are my favorite.

For those who had a preference, the most popular positions are:

32% woman on top

man on top 34%

doggie style 30%

few chose spooning 4%

men prefer doggie style

women prefer men on top

In terms of differences between the genders, college men say their favorite position is doggie style (41% men vs. 26% women), whereas college women say their favorite is having the man on top (39% women vs. 19% men).

How often do you reach orgasm?

College students were asked, "How often do you achieve orgasm during sex with someone?"
Responses ranged from always to never.

most women
do not reach orgasm
through intercourse

For those who have had sex, only one in five (20%) say they always reach orgasm. Slightly more than a third (37%) say they reach orgasm most of the time, while 15% say half the time. The rest say they reach orgasm rarely (16%) or never (12%).

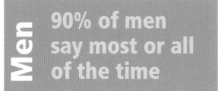

Men
90% of men say most or all of the time

When looking at the differences between women and men, college men are much more likely to say they reach orgasm most or all the time (90%). **On the other hand, more than half the women say they don't usually reach orgasm (55%). In fact,** a third of college women (36%) say they rarely or never reach orgasm with sex. The reality is many women do not reach orgasm through intercourse.

Are you satisfied?

College students were asked, "Are you satisfied with the amount of sex you are having?"

 **66% said yes**

Most sexually active college students say they are satisfied (66%). However, when looking at the gender differences, college men are more likely than women to say they are not satisfied (44% of men vs. 31% of the women). Nearly half of the men are looking for more.

However:

 **44% of men say they are not satisfied**

 **31% of women say they are not satisfied**

Conclusion

What these results confirm is that college is a learning experience in more ways than one. College is not just about academics. Students are on a journey to learn not only about a specific career area, but to learn more about themselves, to discover themselves. They are exposed to new ideas and a diversity of people with different values and experiences. As the survey results indicate, students become more accepting of others and the range of behaviors. And although most arrive at college having already experienced sexual intercourse, the results indicate that they are engaging in a variety of sexual activities that increase with each year they are enrolled. We have a responsibility to prepare them so that they can make informed choices.

The results suggest many positive changes have taken place in the past 25 years in such areas as use of birth control and condoms, and the resulting decline in unplanned pregnancies, abortions and STIs. Women are more in tune with their own pleasure. And we have also seen dramatic changes in attitudes, with an accelerated acceptance of such behaviors as oral and anal sex, as well as greater acceptance and understanding of sexual diversity for people who are lesbian and gay. And while love may be endangered (less than half of today's college students think it's important), it is not extinct.

On the other hand, some things have not necessarily changed at all (e.g., he says he almost always reaches orgasm with sex, while she says she usually does not), or have not changed for the better. While prior generations tended to believe sex was something you did for enjoyment with someone who was important to you or whom you at least liked, now it appears to be something you just do. Contemporary terms like "hooking up" and "friends with benefits" suggest new sexual behaviors for today's college students, but 25 years ago, it was simply called "casual sex." There has not been a rise in the percentage of college students having multiple (5 or more) partners. What has changed is that, by referring to casual sex as "friends with benefits," today's college women are able to participate in what used to be seen as a male-dominated world of casual sex. As they have learned from Facebook, a friend is no longer someone you need to know intimately.

Many of today's entering college students have not been educated in a critical area of their lives — the sexual part. What "sex education" they might have received has too often been too little, too late — and too biological. And for over a quarter century, our country has spent more than $1.5 billion on abstinence-only-until-marriage "education" instead of focusing on providing healthy, comprehensive sexuality education. (I am for "just say no," as long as it's spelled K-N-O-W.) Along with the push for abstinence-only education came the rise in virginity pledges and virginity balls with their specific focus on girls' virginity — not boys'. It is hard to understand how we reached the point where we judge a girl's character by what is between her legs more than what is between her ears and in her heart. It is an indication the sexual double standard is still alive and well. The survey results suggest this double standard as well when we see such results across 25 years revealing:

- A college woman is more likely to say she has had fewer partners, while a man is more likely to say he has been with a higher number (slut vs. stud).
- If virginity matters, she is more likely to say she wants a partner who is experienced; he is more likely to say he wants a virgin.
- In terms of the importance of love and sex, she is more likely to say love is important; he is not. (What is important to him is if he is attracted.)
- A college woman is more likely to believe her parents would be opposed to the idea of her having sex, while a college man is more likely to think his parents (especially dad) would be in favor of it.

At the same time that these college students have been raised with the "just say no" abstinence-only message, they have been surrounded by the "just say yes" influence of living in a highly sexualized society, where exposure to adult-oriented sexually explicit material (e.g., pornography) is a mouse click away. So much of their sex education has been left to chance, uneducated peers and the Internet, resulting in many young people having unrealistic expectations of sex and arriving at college with many misconceptions. The survey findings reveal that some college students today are simply performing sex. Without the proper guidance of their parents and schools, many young people have been misled by the acting world of pornography, which is designed to be stimulating fantasy for adults. Somewhere along the line, we forgot to tell our young people that it is not intended to be sex instruction. But for too many young people, it serves as their primary foundation for sexuality education.

I see this reflected in my survey results that show that across 25 years, faking orgasm by both women and men is on the rise.

The prevalence of faking orgasm among today's college students indicates a real difference between what is happening and what the person thinks should be happening.

The reality versus the fantasy. Orgasm is something they have, not something they feel. At the same time there has been a rise in faking orgasm, the importance of love has dropped way off.

In addition, most young people today shave all their pubic hair, emulating what they see in porn. And a growing number of college women say they engage in same-sex eroticism for the viewing pleasure of their boyfriends. Sex now seems to be about how one appears, as many young women wonder what's wrong if they don't have simultaneous, multiple, g-spot orgasms with their "friend with benefits." At the same time, my survey has found that an increasing number of students are not concerned at all about HIV, and while most college students support abortion, there is a growing percentage who are ambivalent about a woman's right to choose.

We are sex saturated and sex silent. We are more interested in the morality than the reality of sex. Too many people in this country think withholding information and access to services will lead to responsible behavior. As other countries have shown so clearly — Denmark, Finland, France, Germany, The Netherlands and Sweden, to name a few — this is not true and does not work. We need to begin by educating.

We teach the 3 R's (reading, writing, arithmetic) in school. I feel there should be a 4th R: relationships. For the most part, that's what sexuality education is all about. We need to help college students learn what it means to create an intimate relationship, rather than using sex as a way to avoid intimacy.

We need to help them shift from the performance model to one based in pleasure and connection. Instead of judging sex by the number of orgasms, help them judge it by how much pleasure has been created. Instead of asking, "How am I doing?" we need to help college students ask, "Am I enjoying myself?" and "Are we enjoying each other?"

We teach the 3 R's (reading, writing, arithmetic) in school. I feel there should be a 4th R: relationships.

How can we ever become a sexually healthy society if colleges do not educate the future teachers, doctors, lawyers, television producers and, most of all, parents? There is a real need for courses in human sexuality at all levels.

We need to focus more on real sex (the reality of what is happening in people's lives) versus reel sex (the image of what is supposedly going on via what is fed to us through the media).

This survey was designed to give us a glimpse into the lives of college students. We can begin to help by understanding their attitudes and behaviors past and present — where they have been and where they are now.

We need more honest discussions about the role of sexuality in people's lives.

It is hoped that The Sex Lives of College Students can start that dialogue.

We need more public discussions of private parts.

For more information:
thesexlivesofcollegestudents.com

About the Author

Dr. Sandra L. Caron is Professor of Family Relations and Human Sexuality at the University of Maine, where she teaches both undergraduate and graduate courses in family studies and human sexuality. She has been a member of the American Association of Sex Educators, Counselors, and Therapists, and The Society for the Scientific Study of Sexuality for over 30 years. She is the founder and director of three nationally recognized peer sexuality education programs: Athletes for Sexual Responsibility, Male Athletes Against Violence, and The Greek Peer Educator Program. For two decades, she wrote a weekly newspaper column and hosted a radio show on sexuality called "Sex Matters." She now hosts a national website for college students — collegesextalk.com.

Dr. Caron received a Ph.D. in human development with an emphasis in human sexuality in 1986 from Syracuse University, where she studied under Dr. Sol Gordon, along with Dr. Clive Davis. She returned to her home state of Maine and joined the University of Maine faculty in 1988.

Her research and publications have focused on the social-sexual development of young people, with an emphasis on sexual decision-making, contraceptive use, safer sex, sexual assault, sexuality education, and cross-cultural perspectives. She has authored two books published by Pearson, *Sex Matters for College Students: FAQs in Human Sexuality* and *Sex Around the World: Cross-Cultural Perspectives in Human Sexuality.*

Dr. Caron was received numerous recognitions for her work. Most recently, she received the 2013 Lifetime Achievement Award from the Mabel Wadsworth Women's Health Center in Bangor, Maine, for her contribution to the field of sexual and reproductive health. In 2002, she received the University of Maine Presidential Public Service Achievement Award and, in 1999, the Margaret Vaughn Award from the Family Planning Association of Maine, for her outstanding contribution to sexuality education. She received UMaine's 1998 Presidential Outstanding Teaching Award and, in 1997, was the first recipient of the university's Faculty-Student Centered Award. ■

Contributors to
The Sex Lives of College Students

Foreword

CLIVE M. DAVIS taught at Syracuse University from 1967-2005. His research focused on sexuality and communication. He was the founding president of the Foundation for the Scientific Study of Sexuality and has been a member of its Board of Directors since 1985. He was first elected to the Board of Directors of the Society for the Scientific Study of Sexuality in 1976 and has served on one or more SSSS committees continuously ever since. He was as the Editor-in-Chief of *The Journal of Sex Research* from 1977-87, the President of SSSS in 1984-85, and the Associate Editor of the *Annual Review of Sex Research* from its inception through 2008. He also served on the Board of Directors of the Sex and Information Council of the United States and the American Association of Sexuality Educators, Counselors, and Therapists. He co-edited the *Handbook of Sexuality-Related Measures* (3rd edition, 2001).

Statistician

BRIAN DOORE is the Director of Assessment at the University of Maine. He taught assessment and statistics for the UMaine College of Education and Human Development, and has specialized in translating statistically and practically relevant data patterns and trends into understandable language for members of the general public.

Designer/Illustrator

VAL IRELAND is the Manager of Creative Services and Senior Designer at the University of Maine. Her work has garnered numerous graphic design awards throughout her career. The most notable have been national honors including Gold, Silver, Bronze and honorable mentions in the *New York Times*-sponsored Marketing and Promotion Awards Competition for UMaine summer poster illustrations. Consecutive awards have been garnered for more than a dozen years.

Made in the USA
Charleston, SC
10 April 2015